Write a list of adjectives, from A-Z, that describe you as a professional.

Make a list of 5 career objectives that you want to achieve in the next year.

List the people famous or otherwise you would like to have dinner with and discuss your career path.

Make a list of 5 ways to impress your boss this month.

List things you could change to improve the image your job performance invokes.

Make a list of the apps you use the most for your career.

List your feelings about your current work/life balance.

_____
_____
_____
_____
_____
_____
_____
_____
_____
_____
_____
_____
_____
_____
_____
_____
_____
_____
_____

Make a list of 5 ways you can make your work flow better.

List your training and development needs.

Make a list of your biggest career mentors.

Make a list 5 ways you can improve your customers experience.

List ways you can help develop your co-workers.

Make a list of your biggest stress factors relating to your job.

Create a bucket list of your immediate and long-range career goals.

Think of a problem at your office. List ways to solve it.

Make a list of bad career habits you want to avoid.

Make a list of risks you've taken in your career so far.

Make a list of 5 ways you can increase your job satisfaction.

List 5 changes you would make if you could switch positions with your boss.

Make a list of business industry blogs you follow.

Make a list of the business leaders of in the world you admire.

Make a list of the things and experiences you're grateful for in your career journey.

Make a list of adjectives that describe your professional personality.

Make a list of everyone that has influenced you to follow your dreams

_____

_____

_____

_____

_____

_____

_____

_____

_____

_____

_____

_____

_____

_____

_____

_____

_____

_____

Make a list of your daily work routine.

Make a list of your personal business secrets.

Make a list of 10 things that have surprised you about being in your industry.

Make list of your proudest career related moments.

Make a list of your disappointments in your job.

Think of your biggest career goal. List 5 reasons you want to accomplish it.

Make a list of your favorite business quotes.

List the things that make you happy relating to your career.

Make a list of all the work things you're good at.

Make a list of how your job would look if it were easy.

Make a list of issues and problems that concern your career.

Keep an hourly log of what you do on a typical work day.

List 5 things you want to be known for in your career.

Make a list of your career achievements.

Make a list of ways you can continue your career education.

List all the goals you have for your career for this year.

Make a list of the things you intend for your career

Revise your daily routine list for what it should be, so you can be more productive.

Make a list of 5 new ways to improve your work performance this month

Keep a list of the best business books you read throughout the year.

Make a list of all the things you need to get done this week.

Make a list of business qualities you would like to develop in yourself.

___

Make a list describing how your job would be if it were exactly as you wanted.

Make a list of important lessons you've learned pursuing your career.

_____
_____
_____
_____
_____
_____
_____
_____
_____
_____
_____
_____
_____
_____
_____
_____
_____
_____
_____
_____

List ways you could help make your boss's life easier.

Make a list of actions you can take to reach a particular career goal

List all the things you've done this week for your career.

Make a list of things your job needs from you this week

www.ingramcontent.com/pod-product-compliance
Lightning Source LLC
Chambersburg PA
CBHW030513220526
45464CB00006B/2777